the origin
of lament

the origin of lament

by emma magenta

RANDOM HOUSE AUSTRALIA

Random House Australia Pty Ltd
Level 3, 100 Pacific Highway, North Sydney, NSW 2060
www.randomhouse.com.au

Sydney   New York   Toronto
London   Auckland   Johannesburg

First published by Random House Australia 2007

National Library of Australia
Cataloguing-in-Publication Entry

       Magenta, Emma.
       The origin of lament.

       ISBN 978 1 74166 701 1 (pbk).

       I. Title.

       A823.4

Book design by Tim Clift

Printed and Bound in China by 1010 Printing International Limited

10 9 8 7 6 5 4 3 2 1

for louise blue
...thanks for being a font of sanity
during life's muito tricky moments.

x

acknowledgements

big thankyou to jeanne ryckmans.
your faith in my work brought this book into being.

thanks to my editor, brandon van over, and his wonderful
input and enthusiasm, and to all at random house who have
in some way brought this book to fruition.

thanks to tim clift at swell for designing my book again with
the astute awareness of how simplicity equals beauty.
also thanks aaron cuneo for your assistance as well.

thanks to my agent, al zuckerman, for your support
of my work and for keeping the faith.

for btg who made it all happen in the first place.

thanks especially to my beloved arturo aguirre for
supporting me in every way and generally for being
extremely funny at times (fool).

to my dear family for your continual support...thankyou!

thanks to the berkelouw family (especially paul)
for supporting my work for 10 years.

and to these cherubs, whose friendship has inspired
my work: orlando, rakkers, sonia, abi, simon, maggie,
detty, maxine, sophie, ginny, liza, rachel, deb bibby,
becky, budda, all my mates at capoeira brasil — in
particular julio (forminha), gilmara, agua, peixe,
meirde, mariana, galo, and de ouro.

a girl called magenta had procured for herself
the joy of many things.

a cluster of sentient beings gathered
about her as comrades,

Sylvie

as did a small orphaned chicken
by the name of sylvie.

a romantic
union,
free from
the shackles
of artifice,
had also
managed to
find her,

he was
super
real

and to the
envy of several
obsessive folk,
she held down
a greatly
coveted job
as a horse
whisperer.

all that
mattered
to her
was the
pony

with such
a boon of
plenty to
her name, it
could only
be presumed
that she
should feel
glorious
about what
appeared to
be the summit
of personal
fortune.

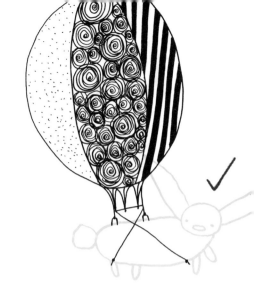

had not an avalanche of adversity befallen her,
perhaps her bubble of delight could have free-floated,
unhindered by the woe of fate.

but, much to her chagrin, that was not to be her story.

the
big joy
exit

as to be expected in any relationship when things are going well, a destiny greater than the two of them awaited her beloved.

an adventure was involved,

as were some friends,

and the promise of unprecedented glory, their goal.

godspeed!

i'll be
back

not wishing to hinder his quest for immortality,
she waved adieu!

with a
courageous
promise to grow
a beard until
he returned, as
an expression of
her faith.

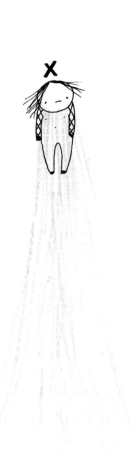

quickly, she turned to her
posse of friends to organise a
coup on disappointment,

i'm
busy
busy
busy

only to discover that her sense of joy was to be
further thwarted by a sudden fellowship drought.

bye

hiding
away

visibly crestfallen, she looked to
her workplace for solace,

they begged for her warm touch

press here to tame wild horse

discovering that it too had an expiration date
in the face of economic rationalism.

suddenly everything that had once seemed certain was now a myth, as it occurred to her that the fabric of her world was fragile,

and,
to say the least,
torn
apart

easy to snag.

stripped of all her reference points, she stood alone,

like a winter tree in a forgotten field.

echo

echo

echo

a monastery of silence now replaced her
much-loved bossa nova as a personal beat.

for a quick moment, heavy metal made sense,

as did the motion to record her angst in
the form of tribal body art,

but to the joy of passers-by,
those feelings passed as quickly as they arose.

in the absence of all she loved, a sudden epiphany
suggested that she now had little clue who she was,

even her
dress
was
confused

and an ill-fated fashion purchase seemed
to support this discovery.

so before she could set up a chaise lounge in the lobby of despair, she escaped her sad, confused self to find out where her joyous self might now be hiding.

the path of cosmic jokes

sporting a countenance of guileless expectation, she
made her way to the promised path to bliss,

and like a beacon, it wasn't long before she
was spotted on the road by several experts
suggesting they knew the way.

the first one
kindly suggested
that to find her
joyous self, she
must look inside
her head to
unlock her past.

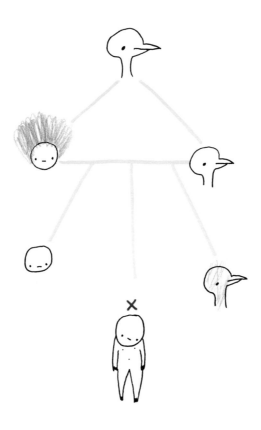

but after much excavation, all that was gleaned from the experience – other than the discovery that she was a direct descendant of a rare bird –

was a storehouse
of unexplored grief and rage,

so mammoth in proportions that to release it would cause a panic in her immediate environment.

so she shut the door on it.

freud
and
jung
wept

with deep fervour, she embraced the
next expert suggestion that declared
that her joyous self was to be
located by looking to the future.

she let go
of her
inherited
thoughts

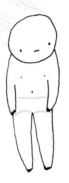

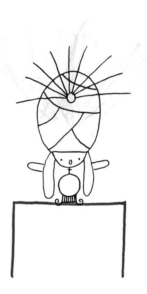

so she consulted a local soothsayer,

she held
on tight
until her
arm
broke

who reassured her that the bliss she longed for was
only 7 years away, and to hang in there.

WANT

THE NEED FILL

require

essentialHAVE

frustrated by
the wait, she
heeded the
counsel
of some
well-placed
billboards,

which lusciously
suggested her
joyous self was
to be found in
the acquisition of
some little winter
shorts,

a range of useless accessories,

and a brand-new face.

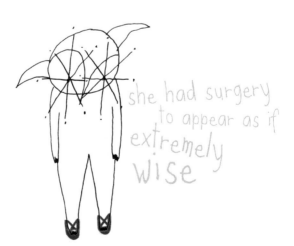

she had surgery
to appear as if
extremely
wise

suddenly having an
owl face
was very
last week

unfortunately, by the end of the week the items
were redundant, so she had to start again.

feeling far from ecstatic
and at the crest of
vulnerability, she reached
out to a passing group of
like-minded others,

help

where she quickly found herself in a circle
exploring song,

and the healing properties
of working with clay.

she
shook

dance,

she had a
shamanic
experience

a drum was played,

and before long a revelation was passed that her joyous self vibrated to the number 8.

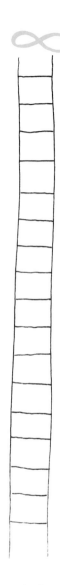

she had only to reach it.

the
infinite
search

she left
it all
behind

with such a
tangible answer
laid out before
her, she let go
of all extraneous
concerns to
concentrate on
how to reach
such a goal,

and before long she was spotted
wearing a hemp smock,

some simple bedouin sandals,

and frequenting a favourite mountain top,
as she looked to the east for guidance.

soy
past life therapy
workshops
tm
firewalking
crystals
bowel cleansing
primal screaming
power walking wheatgrass
psychodrama
pyramid selling therapy
pilates
6 glasses of water a day
aura cleansing
rolfing

for several years she downloaded all the fodder that
assured ascension to her goal,

and
although
she was
stuffed to
the brim with
bach flowers,
crystals and
insights,
she was still
far from the
infinite joy
that was
promised.

she wept soy tears

fresh out of any notion of what to do, she
wandered aimlessly until she came unexpectedly
face to face with her sad, confused self.

she quickly looked for an exit,

but all the doors were locked.

so she placed the sad self in a box
so she couldn't see it,

but she could still hear it weeping, so she let it out.

she turned up the music to drown out its sobbing,

but it wept so much that she almost drowned.

so before she lost her mind completely, she
realised that she had only one course of action:

she decided to just let it say its piece.

after the emotional anarchy had finally ceased,
she held it,

fed it,

and took it for a walk,

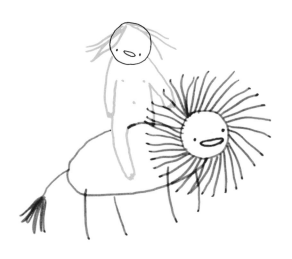

and to her surprise, for the first time
in many years, they both laughed.

joy
restored.

✓